Just For Fun
BENNETT CERF

Just For Fun
BENNETT CERF

* * *

A Collection of Bennett Cerf's Best Stories

STANYAN BOOKS

RANDOM HOUSE

A Stanyan book
Published by Stanyan Books,
8721 Sunset Blvd., Suite C
Hollywood, California 90069,
and by Random House, Inc.
201 East 50th Street,
New York, N.Y. 10022

Library of Congress
Catalog Card Number:
71-157399

Printed in U.S.A.

Designed by Hy Fujita

A NOTE FROM AN INTERESTED PARTY

Having groaned endlessly, before and after dinner, at Mr. Cerf's "quips", I have occasionally laughed in spite of myself.

I am only too pleased to write a word or two in praise of my publisher, Bennett Cerf. He is a gentle man, a kind man, and I love him in spite of his jokes.

I only hope in this book he has not once again been trapped by his own words. If so, I'll go his bail, though I want no part in any law suits involving the estate of Joe Miller.

—Rod McKuen, 1971

In Africa, three big-game hunters were resting by their campfire when one announced, "I'm restless. Think I'll go for a short hike." The other two didn't fret over his non-appearance for an hour. Then one glanced at his watch and murmured, "Hmm! Wonder what's eating old Ernest!"

Mrs. Bemish called to her husband, "Last Christmas we sent Mother a chair. What do you think we ought to do for her this year?" Mr. Bemish called back, "Electrify it."

Consider the case of the hen that observed the undisciplined behavior of her youngest chick with obvious disapproval. "If your father could see you now," she cackled disgustedly, "he'd turn over in his gravy."

"Not a thing to worry about. You can stop trembling," a dentist advised a timorous patient. "I won't have to extract a single tooth." Then he added, "Of course, I'll have to take out the gums."

One big Hollywood producer came home to find his wife sobbing uncontrollably. "That famous author of yours!" she wailed. "He came marching in this afternoon, seized me in his arms, and despite my protests, made violent love to me for three hours." "Hm-m-m," mused the producer, "I wonder what the so-and-so wants?"

A Chinese father summoned his four sons and addressed them thus: "Honorable sons, which one of you sullied the honor of our family by pushing outhouse in creek?"

Number two son bowed ceremoniously and admitted, "Honorable Father, I cannot tell a lie. I pushed outhouse in creek." Number two son thereupon received the beating of his life.

At the conclusion of the whomping, bruised number two son said, "Honorable father, must point out that great President George Washington's father never beat son for telling truth. Is not so?"

"Is indeed so," agreed the father, "but big difference should be noted: great President George Washington's father not sitting in cherry tree."

All the puppies in an Alaskan city recently were expelled. Ever since, it's been known as Dogless Fairbanks!

Two lifelong denizens of a lunatic asylum were engaged in a solemn conclave. "I have decided to conquer England," declared one. "Historians will never be able to say that Julius Caesar rested on his laurels." "England, eh?" mused the other. "Well, Julius, if I were you—and incidentally, I am..."

An English author broke off his lecture tour in Iowa. "I never minded people looking at their watches while I talked," he told his agent, "but out there, they shake them."

That traveling salesman you've always heard about ran out of gas one evening on a lonely road and asked at the only farmhouse in sight (where else?), "Can you put me up for the night?" The farmer said, "I reckon I can — if you don't mind sharing a room with my young son." "Good heavens," gasped the salesman, "I'm in the wrong joke!"

A lovely German fraulein in Washington was suspected of some hanky-panky with government officials. So an investigator asked her if she'd ever been away on trips with senators. "Nein," she said indignantly — and was deported.

A kangaroo yanked her young one out of her pouch and gave it a healthy smack on the backside. "I'll teach you," she declared, "to eat crackers in bed!"

A worker in a violin repair shop claims he restrings an average of fourteen instruments a day. "And that, gentlemen," he adds, "takes guts!"

Is your minister inclined to make his sermons too lengthy? Remind him of this story of Mark Twain's: "I once heard a preacher who was powerful good. I decided to give him every cent I had with me. But he kept at it too long. Ten minutes later I decided to keep the bills and just give him my loose change. Another ten minutes and I was darned if I'd give him anything at all. Then when he finally stopped, and the plate came around, I was so exhausted, I extracted two dollars out of sheer spite."

A missionary and a lion met in the jungle. Flight was out of the question; the missionary sank to his knees in prayer. To his astonishment, the lion did likewise.

"How miraculous," babbled the missionary, "to join you in prayer when just a moment ago I gave myself up for lost!"

"Quiet," ordered the lion. "I'm saying grace."

From a Bob Benchley monologue: "While rummaging through a bureau drawer, I came across some old snow."

A shoestore clerk nominated one customer as the woman in town who has suffered most for her unshakeable belief — her belief that she can put a size 7 foot into a size 4 shoe.

A lobster strolled into a restaurant and sat down at a table. "What would you like, sir?" asked a waiter, and the lobster answered, "A little mayonnaise."

A famous movie star whose name had been coupled for romantic interludes with every beauty in Hollywood entered a Long Island hospital for a check-up and was fawned upon and babied by every nurse in the institution.

One particularly attractive nurse was at his side, it seemed, every time he stirred. When he finally indicated that he'd like to be alone for just a little while, she told him, "Now if you want anything at all, you need only pull this cord."

He gave her his patented irresistible smile and said, "Thank you, my dear. What is the cord attached to?" She smiled back and answered, "Me."

A beautiful young lady tugged constantly at her dress and wiggled uncomfortably. Obviously, a chafing dish!

The morning after their return from a blissful honeymoon, the bridegroom awakened his wife with a bed tray holding a glass of fresh orange juice, fried eggs, crisp bacon, toast and coffee. "See what I've done?" asked the bridegroom. "Every single thing, you darling boy," she cooed. "Good," he grunted. "That's the way I want it every morning."

When Mr. Bauman had to go to London on business, he persuaded his brother to take care of his Siamese cat while he was away. Mr. Bauman dearly loved that Siamese cat, but the brother definitely did not. The very moment Bauman set foot back at Kennedy Airport, therefore, he phoned his brother to check on his cat's health. The brother announced curtly, "Your cat died" — and hung up.

For days Mr. Bauman was inconsolable. Finally, however, he phoned his brother again to point out, "It was needlessly cruel and sadistic of you to tell me bluntly that my poor, poor cat had passed away." "What did you expect me to do?" demanded the brother. "You could have broken the bad news gradually," grumbled Bauman. "First, you could have said the cat was playing on the roof. Later you could have called to say he fell off. The next morning you could have reported he had broken his leg. Then, when I came to get him, you could have told me he had passed away during the night. Well — you didn't have it in you to be that civilized. Now tell me — how's Mama?"

The brother pondered momentarily, then announced, "She's playing on the roof."

A few of those youngsters' letters home from camp to mythical parents:

1. "Dear Mom: Last night a mad hermit killed all the kids. Your late son, Putney."

2. "I got fined for being late to breakfast this morning. I guess I overwashed. Love, Nancy."

3. "Dear Dad: We took a couple of long hikes this week. Please send my other sneaker. Donald."

4. "Dear Folks: What is an epidemic? Love, Tom."

I always have laughed at (1) the man who heard a square-jawed female announce: "I'm a little stiff from lacrosse," and answered understandingly, "Ah, Wisconsin," and (2) the son of a prominent New York editor who was asked by his teacher to name two ancient sports, and came up with "Anthony and Cleopatra."

A worried dog owner demanded of a busy vet, "What should I do if my dog has ticks?" The vet dismissed him with, "Don't wind him!"

That hubbub in a honeymoon hideaway ensued when the bride cooked her first dinner and her husband judged it, "Okay in its way, darling, but it will never take the place of food."

An eligible lass from Siam
Informed a new suitor, Khayam,
"To possess me, of course,
You will have to use force:
Thank heaven you're stronger than I am!"

Once upon a time a reform mayor of Gotham initiated a big clean-up campaign. One of his stints was to set up a special trash can in Times Square and wire it for sound. A small transmitter-receiver was hidden in the can, with an operator with a mike stationed in a window overlooking the square.

Several intrigued reporters were watching when a lady threw an old newspaper on the sidewalk. The trash can admonished her, "That's not the way to keep New York clean, lady. What's your name?" The lady shot one startled look at the can, then snapped, "I don't talk to trash cans" — and strode away.

During World War II, a newly camouflaged destroyer darted out of a British port to escort an American battleship into Plymouth Harbour. The destroyer zigzagged back and forth in the path of the battleship and then signaled by blinker, "What do you think of our camouflage?" The exasperated captain of the battleship signaled back, "It's magnificent. Where the hell are you?"

It was Adlai Stevenson who pointed out, "The relationship of the toastmaster to the speaker should be the same as that of the fan to the fan dancer. It should call attention to the subject without making any particular effort to cover it."

"Gee, Pop," implored a youngster. "Why can't I go out in the green fields and play and run around like all other boys?" The father's terse reply was, "Shut up and deal!"

A girl rushed into a drugstore and asked, "Have you anything for ants?" "You bet," answered the clerk. "Where you got 'em?"

One thing you'll have to concede to a wolf: he whistles while he works.

From a customer in a branch post office: "This package contains a very fragile vase, so please throw it underhand."

There was a little girl in Barcelona, Spain, named Carmen Cohen. Her mother called her Carmen, but her father, for reasons only he could explain, always hailed her by her last name, Cohen. As a result, by the time the unfortunate little girl had reached the age of twelve, she didn't know whether she was Carmen or Cohen.

Perkins was twenty minutes late at the first tee one Sunday morning, and the other three members of the regular foursome were almost ready to drive off without him. "I agreed with my wife," explained Perkins, "that this Sunday I'd toss to see whether I played golf or went to church. And you know, fellows, I had to toss twenty-four times."

A wife suggested to her husband, "Let's buy Junior a bicycle." "Do you think it might improve his behavior?" asked the ever-hopeful husband. "I do not," admitted the wife, "but at least it will spread it over the neighborhood."

A thoughtful pediatrician reminded a comparatively new father, "Never spank your child on an empty stomach. Be sure to eat something first." Then he noticed that the baby's hair had turned white. "This kid worrying about something?" he asked. "It's not the kid at all," the father answered him. "It's my near-sighted wife. She keeps powdering the wrong end."

There's an elegant gentleman in Los Angeles who's an absolute whiz at repairing broken pipes and clogged sinks, but who definitely does NOT like being called a plumber. His business card reads, "Hiram Blank, DRAIN SURGEON!" Incidentally, he won't make house calls!

During the filming of a shoestring production in a Kansas town, the director dreamed up a method for getting a realistic street fight at virtually no expense. "See that couple coming down the avenue?" he asked the leading man. "Go up and insult his wife. When her husband winds up to sock you, we'll start the camera rolling."

As instructed, the actor accosted the husband, demanding, "Is this dame your wife?" "She certainly is," bristled the man. "Why?" "Because," sneered the actor, "she's about the homeliest dish I've ever laid eyes on."

This was the moment when the husband turned to his wife and exulted, "See? What did I tell you?"

After an itinerant backwoods preacher had delivered a hell-and-brimstone sermon, he demanded of Deacon Swartbill, "Do you love your neighbor?" "I try to," replied the deacon earnestly, "but she won't let me."

A lady told her new maid, "I declare, I can write my full name in the dust you've left on this piano." "Bless my soul," answered the maid with delight. "It's sure nice to be working for a lady with education!"

A lady who was worried at the failure of her twenty-eight-year-old daughter to find a husband persuaded her to insert a classified ad in the "personal" columns, reading: "Beautiful, exotic young heiress seeks correspondence with devil-may-care gentleman who wants to go places fast." Two days after the ad appeared, the mother asked anxiously, "Well? Any answers?" "Just one," sighed her daughter. "Who wrote it?" demanded Mama. "I can't tell you," said the daughter. "But this was my idea," shouted Mama, "and I insist upon knowing." "All right," said the daughter wearily. "It was Papa."

In Cleveland, a guest conductor was driven crazy at rehearsals because at least one member of the orchestra was always missing. After the last rehearsal, he tapped for attention and said, "I want to thank the first violinist publicly for being the only man in the entire orchestra who had the decency to attend every rehearsal." The first violinist hung his head. "It seemed the least I could do," he said in a deprecating tone. "You see, I don't expect to show up for the concert tonight."

A very stout comedian squeezed himself into one of those horrible new miniature taxicabs and instructed the driver, "Take me to a larger cab."

A doctor examined a very pretty new patient carefully, then beamed, "Mrs. Atherton, I've got good news for you." The patient said, "Pardon me, Doctor; it's MISS Atherton. "Oh," said the doctor. "Well, Miss Atherton, I've got bad news for you."

A sergeant looked over a squad of particularly inept draftees and confessed, "I'm damned if I know what to do with you clumsy goons." One of them piped up hopefully, "There's a big shady tree over there, Sarge." "Yeah, I know," nodded the sergeant, "but I don't have any rope with me."

Two society leaders in Africa's snobbiest cannibal tribe were discussing their marital troubles. "I don't know what to make of my husband these days," confessed the first. "Don't let that bother you," the second reassured her. "I'll send over my new book of recipes."

A Vassar senior told a plastic surgeon she yearned for a "turned up" nose. The doctor turned it up a trifle too far. Now every time the poor girl sneezes she blows her hat off.

If a bakery explodes in your face, what might you see?

A Napoleon blown apart, of course!

Producer Max Gordon instructed his secretary to locate a certain brash comedian who was working on the road. She returned to report, "You're too late. He died last night in Kansas City." To which Gordon sighed, "He always did!"

In Philadelphia, a prosecuting attorney ordered a comely defendant, "Tell the jury just why you shot your husband with a bow and arrow—and remember, you've sworn to tell the truth." The defendant brushed away a tear and answered, "I didn't want to wake the children."

A mink-coated matron ankled into an exclusive Beacon Hill psychiatrist's office leading a duck by a gold chain. "What can I do for you?" asked the psychiatrist. "You can't do anything for me," answered the matron. "It's my poor husband. He seems to think he's a duck."

A Hollywood "wolf" noticed a beautiful girl sitting by herself in a hotel lobby. Infinitely sure of himself, he registered "Mr. So-and-So and wife," and then strolled over to make her acquaintance. Two days later they handed him a bill for six hundred dollars. "What's the idea?" he sputtered. "I've only been here two days." "That's right," said the clerk smoothly, "but your wife has been here for a month and a half."

A team playing baseball in Dallas
Called the umpire blind and of malice.
While the poor ump had fits
The team made eight hits
And a girl in the grandstand named Alice.

A high-falutin' admiral was invited for a hunt on a duke's enormous estate. He reported later that he had brought down one animal the likes of which he never had seen before. "All I can tell you," he added, "is that it had great big shoulders, a long nose, and an enormous rear." "Good heavens," gasped an English journalist, "he's shot the duchess!"

The receipts of a Wall Street bookshop are being swelled by its sale of a volume telling you how to save ninety percent on your income tax. It's packaged with a one-way plane ticket to Tahiti.

An old plutocrat, his wheel chair pulled up to the window of his Fifth Avenue mansion, smacked his lips as a lovely young nursemaid wheeled her charge toward the park entrance. "Quick, Tague," he cried to his butler. "Bring my teeth! I want to whistle."

A persevering couple shrugged off eight successive daughters and finally produced a boy on their ninth try. The delirious father promptly went on a week-long toot that broke several records. On the seventh day, somebody asked him, "Who does it look like, you or your wife?" "I don't know," chortled the proud papa. "We haven't looked at his face yet."

A Maine lobster merchant received an urgent telephone call informing him that the body of his mother-in-law had been cast up by the tide with a lobster firmly attached to each toe. When the Coast Guard asked, "What'll we do with the body?" he answered, "Sell the lobsters and set her out again."

A very ugly girl was sitting alone at the beach, when the waves washed a bottle to her feet. She opened it — and out blew a huge genie in a billow of smoke. "I've been a prisoner in this bottle for five thousand years," cried the genie, "and now you've freed me! As a reward, I will fulfill any wish you make." Ecstatic, the ugly girl announced, "I want a figure like Sophia Loren, a face like Elizabeth Taylor, and legs like Ginger Rogers." The genie looked her over carefully, then sighed, "Baby, just put me back in the bottle!"

A merchant from Minsk drove his horse and loaded wagon to a neighboring town and was asked by a prospective customer, "What are you selling today?" The merchant whispered in his ear, "Oats." "Why the secrecy?" demanded the customer. "S-s-sh," soothed the merchant. "Not so loud. I don't want the horse to hear."

A lady went running to a doctor with a badly spoiled stomach. "What did you eat for dinner last night?" asked the doctor. "Oysters," she said. "Fresh oysters?" asked the doctor. "How should I know?" said the lady. "Well," asked the doctor, "couldn't you tell when you took off the shells?" "My God," gasped the lady. "Are you supposed to take off the shells?"

A shoddy trick was played on a prospective benedict in Chicago recently. He passed out cold at his bachelor party. When he came to, his right arm was in a cast. He had broken it, they told him, in a battle royal. The poor victim spent his entire honeymoon with a perfectly good arm in a tight cast.

In a poker game, a henpecked husband turned out to be the only winner. He didn't like to quit when he was so far ahead, but as the hours went by, he grew visibly more apprehensive. Suddenly, at about 2:20 A.M. he had an inspiration. He called his wife on the phone and when she answered, he cried to her, "Don't pay the ransom, darling. I've escaped."

A celebrated swami had a cousin who, understandably enough, was a whirling dervish in the Ringling Circus. One day an uncommonly handsome damsel picked up this dervish and took him out for a row on the lake in Central Park.

Suddenly the boat tilted, and the damsel quavered to her companion, "I'm afraid I've lost my oar, Derv."

Just after a famous cruise ship sailed one blowy afternoon, she ran into a full gale. The dozen Very Important Persons who had been assigned to the captain's table appeared for dinner amidst definite signs of distress. The captain cleared his throat and spoke as follows:

"I hope the twelve of you will enjoy your trip. It is a pleasure to look into your eleven faces and realize that the eight of us will be dining together for the next few evenings. If any of the four of you would like a rubber of bridge, I'll be glad to see you both in my cabin. Waiter, I dislike dining alone, so I will dispense with the rest of my dinner."

One of Groucho Marx's most famous rejoinders was made when a friend stopped short on Sunset Boulevard and exclaimed, "I must find a Western Union office. I've got to wire my father." "What's the matter?" demanded Groucho. "Can't he stand up by himself?"

A prominent Wall Street banker was leaving his home in White Plains to catch the 9:15 when his wife called out, "Please take my shoes and leave them at the Grand Central repair shop on your way to the office." The banker took the shoes under his arm without bothering to wrap them, and swung aboard the train with his mind teeming with details of million-dollar deals. A fellow commuter noted the shoes and boomed enthusiastically, "That's the way to do it, Joe. Don't let her gad about."

A junior clerk in the American Embassy was entertained by a duchess at one of the stately homes of England. Upon his return to his quarters, everybody was agog for details. "Well," he drawled, "if the water had been as cold as the soup, and if the soup had been as warm as the wine, and if the wine had been as old as the chicken, and if the chicken had been as young as the maid, and if the maid had been as willing as the duchess—I probably never would have come home at all."

A reporter who was doing a feature story on Madame Tussaud's Wax Works in London sought out the laundress who had washed for the exhibition for twenty-five years.

"Tell me," said the journalist. "Do the queens and the duchesses in the wax works wear anything under those gorgeous velvet robes?"

"As a matter of fact, they don't," the laundress admitted. "But I'd rather you didn't make it public. As it is, nobody knows but me and a few Australian soldiers!"

A flutist at the Berkshire Music Festival figured in a famous Toscanini episode. The maestro interrupted a rehearsal to upbraid the unfortunate fellow and ended by firing him on the spot. The departing flutist muttered, "You blank-blank egomaniac. I'd like to..." Toscanini cut in angrily, "No, no! None of your apologies!"

A glamorous young lady hit the jackpot with her very first novel. With part of the proceeds, she indulged a childhood fancy, and had her new boudoir done in bright yellow — yellow drapes, yellow spreads, even yellow silk sheets and pillow cases. To make the picture complete, she was laid low shortly thereafter with a sharp attack of yellow jaundice.

A doctor was summoned but when he entered the lady's boudoir he ran into an unforeseen difficulty.

He couldn't find her.

When 5-year-old Bartholomew came home from kindergarten one day and told his mother he'd like to have a little talk with her about sex, Mom braced herself for a rather difficult session, but bravely asked, "Exactly what is it about sex you'd like me to explain?" "What I want to know," answered Bartholomew, "is am I the opposite sex or is Susan?"

A minor playwright in New York is fond of telling all and sundry about his perpetual hard luck. To emphasize his point, he's created a fantasy wherein the Good Lord asks Gabriel one morning, "What's that fellow doing down there on earth?" Gabriel answers, "He's relaxing on his front lawn, smelling a flower." The Good Lord says, "He is, is he? Well, send down a bee to sting him!"

William Faulkner liked to tell about a ball game once staged in Mississippi. It was staged in a cow pasture and ended abruptly when a runner slid into what he thought was third base.

The evening before their marriage, an ardent suitor told his bashful bride-to-be, "You don't know how to make love, darling. Now tonight I'm going to show you first how Cousin Joe makes love, second how Uncle Louis makes love, and third, how Brother Theodore makes love."

The next morning the young man received a telegram from the girl, reading, "I'm sorry I cannot marry you. Have just eloped with your Uncle Louis."